This journal belongs to:

_____

My first entry: ____ / ____ / _____

My last entry: ____ / ____ / _____

For every traveler who has any taste of his own, the only useful
guidebook will be the one which he himself has written.
—ALDOUS HUXLEY

Arizona Reflections

A TRAVEL JOURNAL

by LINDA KRANZ

photography by KLAUS KRANZ

NORTHLAND PUBLISHING
www.northlandpub.com

For Papa

Text © 2002 by Linda Kranz
Photographs © 2002 by Klaus Kranz
All rights reserved.

www.northlandpub.com

Composed in the United States of America
Printed in Korea

Edited by Tammy Gales
Designed by Jennifer Schaber
Production supervised by Donna Boyd

FIRST PRINTING 2002
ISBN 0-87358-801-0

02 03 04 05 06   5 4 3 2 1

Inquiries about the photography should be addressed to the publisher.

I searched for many months to find a travel journal to take along on our weekend adventures. I came across one or two that had "Travel Journal" neatly written on the cover, but when I opened them, much to my disappointment, all I saw were endless pages of black lines. Sometimes I find it hard to write when all I see are blank pages. I know that inspiring quotes, full-color photography, and a comfortable amount of space to write make all the difference in the world. This journal is designed to incorporate all those features.

I created this journal to be flexible so take some time and glance through the pages. You will find three separate sections that you can chose from when you are going out to explore: Day Trips, Weekend Trips, and Vacations. Within each section I offer ideas to get you writing, but they are merely suggestions.

In the back of the journal, you will find a few helpful facts and references. One section to take note of is the listing of Resources which include contact information for local Chambers of Commerce, State and National Parks, and other tourist related offices. I recommend that you contact these places about a month before you plan to visit that part of the state, as they can send you a wealth of free information. Another page contains a "Check List" of items to bring along on each trip, which you can further personalize to suit your own needs. Lastly, I have included a guide to the average temperatures for both the desert and mountain regions, and to the approximate times of the Arizona sunrise and sunset.

It seems that often during the course of our lives we tend to get busy—so busy, perhaps, that we forget about the things that help us to relax and the things that make us smile. Once you begin filling up the pages of this journal, keep it in a place where it is visible and make time to revisit the "getaways" you have written about. This journal will always be a pleasant reminder. We are almost certain that soon after you have read a few pages, you will be making plans for another trip, packing your suitcases, and creating new memories. Don't forget your journal! And most importantly—be sure to have fun discovering Arizona!

Linda and Klaus Kranz

EVENING THUNDERSTORM, YAVAPAI POINT, GRAND CANYON NATIONAL PARK The Canyon is located about an hour and a half north of Flagstaff. Year round views offer visitors many seasons to enjoy the Grand Canyon.

We do not remember days:
we remember moments.
—CESARE PAVESE

Date_____ Day of the week_____

Time we left_____ When we returned_____

Today we drove to…

Why we wanted to visit this place…

How we heard about it… We've been here before or this is our first time here… The cost of gas…

What was the weather like? Blue skies or cloudy?

Describe the sights, sounds, and "the feel" of this place.

Interesting people we met or unusual things we saw...

How we spent the day...

Momentos or souvenirs we brought home...

The ride home... The next time we come here...

MEXICAN GOLD POPPIES, PICACHO PEAK STATE PARK The park is located forty minutes north of Tucson. Springtime flowers decorate this volcanic landscape with splashes of color each year.

What I will remember most about this day...

We all live under the same sky, but
we don't have the same horizon.
—KONRAD ADENAUER

Put your own photos here or draw something you want to remember.

PROMONTORY BUTTE, MOGOLLON RIM Cool mountain temperatures make a summer's drive along the rim road north of Payson a fun weekend getaway.

Day Trip

Writing gives me an excuse to travel, and travel gives me something to write about.

—ATHENA V. LORD

Date_____ Day of the week_____

Time we left_____ When we returned_____

Today we drove to…

Why we wanted to visit this place…

How we heard about it… We've been here before or this is our first time here… The cost of gas…

Interesting people we met or unusual things we saw…

What was the weather like? Breezy or calm?

Momentos or souvenirs we brought home...

Describe the sights, sounds, and "the feel" of this place.

How we spent the day...

The next time we come here... The ride home...

What I will remember most about this day...

Nature never did betray the heart that loved her.
—WILLIAM WORDSWORTH

EVENING LIGHT AND SUMMER STORM, WHITE MOUNTAINS During the late summer months in the White Mountains, chances are good that you will experience a thunderstorm.

Keep some souvenirs of your past, or how will you ever prove it wasn't all a dream?
—ASHLEIGH BRILLIANT

Date_____ Day of the week_____

Time we left_____ When we returned_____

Today we drove to…

Why we wanted to visit this place…

How we heard about it… We've been here before or this is our first time here… The cost of gas…

What was the weather like? Blue skies or cloudy?

Describe the sights, sounds, and "the feel" of this place.

Interesting people we met or unusual things we saw...

How we spent the day...

Momentos or souvenirs we brought home...

The ride home... The next time we come here...

SUNSET, LAKE POWELL Lake Powell is two hours north of Flagstaff. It offers a unique desert landscape that is accented by reflections across the lake as the sun sets.

What I will remember most about this day...

Adopt the peace of nature; her secret is patience.
—RALPH WALDO EMERSON

CANYON CREEK, MOGOLLON RIM, TONTO NATIONAL FOREST This small, quiet creek is located off Hwy 260, east of Christopher Creek. It is especially calm and picturesque in the spring and fall seasons.

One touch of Nature makes the whole world kin.
—WILLIAM SHAKESPEARE

Day Trip

You lose sight of things... and when you travel, everything balances out.
—DARANNA GIDEL

Date _____ Day of the week _____

Time we left _____ When we returned _____

Today we drove to...

Why we wanted to visit this place...

How we heard about it... We've been here before or this is our first time here... The cost of gas...

Interesting people we met or unusual things we saw...

What was the weather like? Breezy or calm?

Momentos or souvenirs we brought home…

Describe the sights, sounds, and "the feel" of this place.

How we spent the day…

The next time we come here… The ride home…

SUNSET AT YAVAPAI POINT, SOUTH RIM, GRAND CANYON NATIONAL PARK The Canyon is located an hour and a half north of Flagstaff. Find a comfortable place to sit and watch the colors change inside the canyon at sunset.

What I will remember most about this day...

Climb up on some hill at sunrise. Everybody needs
perspective once in a while, and you'll find it there.

—ROBB SAGENDORPH

Day Trip

The world is a book and those
who do not travel read only one page.
— ST. AUGUSTINE

Date_____ Day of the week_____

Time we left_____ When we returned_____

Today we drove to…

Why we wanted to visit this place…

How we heard about it… We've been here before or this is our first time here… The cost of gas…

What was the weather like? Blue skies or cloudy?

Describe the sights, sounds, and "the feel" of this place.

Interesting people we met or unusual things we saw...

How we spent the day...

Momentos or souvenirs we brought home...

The ride home... The next time we come here...

EAST FORK OF THE BLACK RIVER, WHITE MOUNTAINS A short drive from Alpine, the Black River offers many relaxing picnic and camping spots for travelers looking for a quiet, out of the way place.

When there is a river in your growing up, you probably always hear it.

—ANN ZWINGER

Put your own photos here or draw something you want to remember.

What I will remember most about this day…

A road twice traveled is never as long.
—ROSALIE GRAHAM

WUKOKI PUEBLO, WUPATKI NATIONAL MONUMENT Located one hour north of Flagstaff and open all year, this peaceful area with its sweeping views of the painted desert will have your mind wandering back to a different time.

Day Trip

> Because of our routines we forget that
> life is an ongoing adventure.
> —Maya Angelou

Date_____ Day of the week_____

Time we left_____ When we returned_____

Today we drove to…

Why we wanted to visit this place…

How we heard about it… We've been here before or this is our first time here… The cost of gas…

Interesting people we met or unusual things we saw…

What was the weather like? Breezy or calm?

Momentos or souvenirs we brought home…

Describe the sights, sounds, and "the feel" of this place.

How we spent the day…

The next time we come here… The ride home…

What I will remember most about this day…

Take out a map, study it, and then plan a trip to a
place you have never been before. Be adventurous!

—LINDA KRANZ

MEXICAN GOLD POPPIES, SUPERSTITION MOUNTAINS Just north of Apache Junction off Highway 88, this park offers a large variety of trails and colorful wildflowers each spring.

To travel is to take a journey into yourself.
— DENA KAYE

Date_____ Day of the week_____

Time we left_____ When we returned_____

Today we drove to…

Why we wanted to visit this place…

How we heard about it… We've been here before or this is our first time here… The cost of gas…

What was the weather like? Blue skies or cloudy?

Describe the sights, sounds, and "the feel" of this place.

Interesting people we met or unusual things we saw…

How we spent the day…

Momentos or souvenirs we brought home…

The ride home… The next time we come here…

What I will remember most about this day…

FLY AGARIC MUSHROOM, WHITE MOUNTAINS The best time to catch sight of these poisonous mushrooms is in the late summer months.

Nature always tends to act in the simplest way.

— BERNOUILLI

SUNSET, LAKE MARY, FLAGSTAFF Located twenty minutes south of Flagstaff, this lake offers many options for outdoor enthusiasts. Visit the lake in the fall when you can hear the elk bugle just before sunset.

It is the marriage of the soul with Nature
that makes the intellect fruitful, and gives
birth to imagination.

—HENRY DAVID THOREAU

The writer is an explorer. Every step
is an advance into new land.
— RALPH WALDO EMERSON

Date_____ Day of the week_____

Time we left_____ When we returned_____

Today we drove to…

Why we wanted to visit this place…

How we heard about it… We've been here before or this is our first time here… The cost of gas…

Interesting people we met or unusual things we saw…

What was the weather like? Breezy or calm?

Momentos or souvenirs we brought home…

Describe the sights, sounds, and "the feel" of this place.

How we spent the day…

The next time we come here… The ride home…

What I will remember most about this day…

We do not own the land… We hold it in trust for tomorrow.
—Louis L'Amour

Aspens in fall colors, Flagstaff The fall is an amazingly colorful season in the northern areas of Arizona.

COLORADO RIVER, GLEN CANYON The Canyon is two hours north of Flagstaff. High walls and many hiking trails make this a great place to explore during the spring and fall months when temperatures are comfortable.

An original life is unexplored territory.
You don't get there by taking a taxi—you
get there by carrying a canoe.

—ALAN ALDA

Seek out the road less traveled,
and surely you will find peace there.
—LINDA KRANZ

Date_____ Day of the week_____

Time we left_____ When we returned_____

Today we drove to...

Why we wanted to visit this place...

How we heard about it... We've been here before or this is our first time here... The cost of gas...

What was the weather like? Blue skies or cloudy?

Describe the sights, sounds, and "the feel" of this place.

Put your own photos here or draw something you want to remember.

Interesting people we met or unusual things we saw…

How we spent the day…

Momentos or souvenirs we brought home…

The ride home… The next time we come here…

What I will remember most about this day...

The journey is the reward.
—TAOIST SAYING

Day Trip

Adventure is my only reason for living.
— ALEXANDRA DAVID-NEEL

Date_____ Day of the week_____

Time we left_____ When we returned_____

Today we drove to…

Why we wanted to visit this place…

How we heard about it… We've been here before or this is our first time here… The cost of gas…

Interesting people we met or unusual things we saw…

What was the weather like? Breezy or calm?

Momentos or souvenirs we brought home…

Describe the sights, sounds, and "the feel" of this place.

How we spent the day…

The next time we come here… The ride home…

PETROGLYPHS AT RED TANK DRAW Even though you can visit Red Tank Draw all year, the best time to retreat to this captivating area is in the winter.

What I will remember most about this day…

Like all great travelers, I have seen more than I
remember, and remember more than I have seen.
—BENJAMIN DISRAELI

Date _____ Day of the week _____

Time we left _____ When we returned _____

Today we drove to…

Why we wanted to visit this place…

How we heard about it… We've been here before or this is our first time here… The cost of gas…

What was the weather like? Blue skies or cloudy?

Describe the sights, sounds, and "the feel" of this place.

BLUE MESA, PETRIFIED FOREST NATIONAL PARK Located just east of Holbrook off I-40, this colorful desert landscape scattered with petrified trees is an interesting place to visit any time of the year.

Interesting people we met or unusual things we saw…

How we spent the day…

Momentos or souvenirs we brought home…

The ride home… The next time we come here…

LIZARD TRACKS IN SAND DUNES, MONUMENT VALLEY Whether you see lizard tracks or not, this incredible valley will leave you with a feeling of awe.

What I will remember most about this day...

Everything has its beauty but not everyone sees it.

—CONFUCIUS

Put your own photos here or draw something you want to remember.

MONUMENT VALLEY, NAVAJO TRIBAL PARK The Park is located north of Kayenta just off Hwy 163. In this far northern area of the state, a narrow road winds through a colorful landscape and offers year-round spectacular views in all directions.

Day Trip

> Memory is the diary that we
> all carry about with us.
> —Oscar Wilde

Date_____ Day of the week_____

Time we left_____ When we returned_____

Today we drove to…

Why we wanted to visit this place…

How we heard about it… We've been here before or this is our first time here… The cost of gas…

Interesting people we met or unusual things we saw…

What was the weather like? Breezy or calm?

Momentos or souvenirs we brought home...

Describe the sights, sounds, and "the feel" of this place.

How we spent the day...

The next time we come here... The ride home...

What I will remember most about this day…

Go as far as you can see, and when you get there, you can see farther.
—B.J. MARSHALL

CATHEDRAL ROCK, SEDONA Oak Creek is a beautiful place to visit any time of the year, and the state park offers plenty of picnic areas and a wide system of hiking trails.

Weekend Trip

Travel and change of place
impart new vigor to the mind.
—SENECA

Date _____ Day of the week _____

Time we left _____ Time we arrived _____

Time we left for home _____ Time we returned _____

Today we drove to…

Why we wanted to visit this place…

How we heard about it…

We've been here before or this is our first time here…

Why we chose to come here at this time of the year…

Interesting things we saw on our way here…

The terrain we covered… The cost of gas…

Describe the sights, sounds, and "the feel" of the place.

What was the weather like? Blue skies or cloudy?

How we spent our days…

Culinary delights we had for breakfast, lunch, or dinner...

Where we are staying, why we chose to stay here... The view from our window...

The cost per night, the sleeping arrangements...

STRAWBERRY HEDGEHOG CACTUS, BEAVER CREEK This high desert
landscape offers plenty of year-round hiking trails.

Another place or two that we might want to consider staying next time…

Momentos or souvenirs we brought home…

The next time we come here we would like to…

I'm glad I remembered to bring… Next time I don't want to forget…

The ride home…

OCOTILLO IN BLOOM, GATES PASS, TUCSON Most of the year, Ocotillos look like thorny dead sticks, but a rain will bring fresh leaves and beautiful red flowers.

Life in the desert is a wondrous, miraculous thing, but perhaps, the most wondrous and miraculous of all is the transformation of drab desert land into a veritable flower garden when the rains come in the winter and early spring. It doesn't happen every year, but when it does, it's worth waiting and watching for.

—RAYMOND CARLSON

What I will remember most about this getaway…

The language of Nature
is the universal language.
—CHRISTOPH GLUCK

Put your own photos here or draw something you want to remember.

THREE FORKS, WHITE MOUNTAINS This area of the White Mountains near Alpine is lush and green during the late summer months. Wide open spaces abound and there are many opportunities for viewing wildlife.

Climb the mountains and get their good tidings. Nature's peace will flow into you as sunshine flows into trees. The winds will blow their freshness into you, and the storms their energy, while cares will drop off like falling leaves.

—JOHN MUIR

Dreaming is a way of traveling hopefully.
— ELIZABETH DAVID

Date _____ Day of the week _____

Time we left _____ Time we arrived _____

Time we left for home _____ Time we returned _____

Today we drove to…

Why we wanted to visit this place…

How we heard about it…

We've been here before or this is our first time here…

Why we chose to come here at this time of the year…

Interesting things we saw on our way here…

The terrain we covered… The cost of gas…

What was the weather like? Breezy or calm?

Where we are staying, why we chose to stay here… The view from our window…

The cost per night, the sleeping arrangements…

Another place or two that we might want to consider staying next time…

We ate out or made our own recipes…

How we spent our days…

WHEELER THISTLE, WEST FORK OF THE BLACK RIVER It is always worth the drive to this peaceful river, which is host to an abundance of animal and plant life.

Describe the sights, sounds, and "the feel" of the place.

I'm glad I remembered to bring… Next time I don't want to forget…

The next time we come here we would like to…

Momentos or souvenirs we brought home…

The ride home…

SUNSET AT SIGNAL HILL, SAGUARO NATIONAL PARK WEST, TUCSON This year-round short hike will reward you with great views. If you are lucky, you might even hear coyotes serenading the end of the day.

What I will remember most about this getaway…

I am sure that the remainder of our lives will be the richer for our having seen the Grand Canyon.

—JOHN BURROUGHS

A journey of a thousand miles
must begin with a single step.
— LAO-TZE

Date_____ Day of the week_____

Time we left_____ Time we arrived_____

Time we left for home_____ Time we returned_____

Today we drove to…

Why we wanted to visit this place…

How we heard about it…

We've been here before or this is our first time here…

Why we chose to come here at this time of the year…

Interesting things we saw on our way here…

The terrain we covered… The cost of gas…

Describe the sights, sounds, and "the feel" of the place.

What was the weather like? Blue skies or cloudy?

How we spent our days…

SNOW COVER ON AGASSIZ AND FREMONT PEAKS, FLAGSTAFF A hike on the San Francisco Peaks during the spring and summer seasons can offer many picnic opportunities. In the fall, the changing colors will astound you.

I love to trace the silhouette of the mountains with my eyes—the color variations, the details—so I can remember what I saw with complete clarity and recall the peacefulness I found there.

—LINDA KRANZ

Culinary delights we had for breakfast, lunch, or dinner…

Where we are staying, why we chose to stay here… The view from our window…

The cost per night, the sleeping arrangements…

Another place or two that we might want to consider staying next time…

Momentos or souvenirs we brought home…

The next time we come here we would like to…

I'm glad I remembered to bring… Next time I don't want to forget…

The ride home…

SONORAN DESERT LANDSCAPE, GATES PASS, TUCSON In early spring, depending on the amount of rainfall received the previous fall, the desert can turn into a multicolored flower garden.

I noticed immediately a more bracing quality in the air; a cleaner, bluer sky, a more buoyant note in the song of the birds; a snap and sparkle in the air that only Arizona air has, and I said to myself, without reference to a map, that we were now Home.

—BARRY GOLDWATER

What I will remember most about this getaway…

We can never have enough of Nature.
— HENRY DAVID THOREAU

HIGH DESERT VEGETATION, WUPATKI NATIONAL MONUMENT A paved road meanders through the high desert landscape. Each season offers a different view of the San Francisco Peaks.

Clouds that appear around a summer monsoon
will captivate your eyes and your senses and
certainly leave you at a loss for words to describe
the beauty before you.

—LINDA KRANZ

Among my most prized possessions are words that I have never spoken.
— ORSON REGACARD

Date_____ Day of the week_____

Time we left_____ Time we arrived_____

Time we left for home_____ Time we returned_____

Today we drove to...

Why we wanted to visit this place...

How we heard about it...

We've been here before or this is our first time here...

Why we chose to come here at this time of the year...

Interesting things we saw on our way here...

The terrain we covered... The cost of gas...

What was the weather like? Breezy or calm?

Where we are staying, why we chose to stay here… The view from our window…

The cost per night, the sleeping arrangements…

Another place or two that we might want to consider staying next time…

We ate out or made our own recipes…

SAGUARO SILHOUETTES, PICACHO PEAK STATE PARK, TUCSON Colorful sunsets abound in this beautiful, varied landscape.

How we spent our days…

Describe the sights, sounds, and "the feel" of the place.

I'm glad I remembered to bring... Next time I don't want to forget...

The next time we come here we would like to...

Momentos or souvenirs we brought home...

The ride home...

MONTEZUMA CASTLE, MONTEZUMA CASTLE NATIONAL MONUMENT Located a few miles north of Camp Verde, this popular spot offers plenty of shade during the spring, summer, and fall months.

What I will remember most about this getaway…

No, wilderness is not a luxury but a necessity
of the human spirit, as vital to our lives as
water and good bread.

—EDWARD ABBEY

Traveling is like falling in love;
the world is made new.

—JAN MYRDAL

Date _____ Day of the week _____

Time we left _____ Time we arrived _____

Time we left for home _____ Time we returned _____

Today we drove to…

Why we wanted to visit this place…

How we heard about it…

We've been here before or this is our first time here…

Why we chose to come here at this time of the year…

Interesting things we saw on our way here…

The terrain we covered… The cost of gas…

Describe the sights, sounds, and "the feel" of the place.

What was the weather like? Blue skies or cloudy?

How we spent our days…

Culinary delights we had for breakfast, lunch, or dinner…

Where we are staying, why we chose to stay here… The view from our window…

The cost per night, the sleeping arrangements…

IVES MESA, LITTLE PAINTED DESERT The Mesa is located north of Winslow just off Hwy 87. This area offers year-round views of the rich desert landscape.

Commonly we stride through the out-of-doors
too swiftly to see more than the obvious and
prominent things. For observing nature, the best
pace is a snail's pace.

— EDWIN WAY TEALE

Another place or two that we might want to consider staying next time…

Momentos or souvenirs we brought home…

The next time we come here we would like to…

I'm glad I remembered to bring… Next time I don't want to forget…

The ride home…

What I will remember most about this getaway…

When one tugs at a single thing in nature, he
finds it attached to the rest of the world.
—JOHN MUIR

Put your own photos here or draw something you want to remember.

FALL COLORS IN WEST FORK OF OAK CREEK, SEDONA If you haven't hiked through Oak Creek Canyon in the fall, make a point to do so this year. You will be delighted at the variety of colors you will see.

Our happiest moments as tourists always seem to come when we stumble upon something while in pursuit of something else.

— LAWRENCE BLOCK

Traveling… is either an escape or a discovery.
— ROSIE THOMAS

Date _____ Day of the week _____

Time we left _____ Time we arrived _____

Time we left for home _____ Time we returned _____

Today we drove to…

Why we wanted to visit this place…

How we heard about it…

We've been here before or this is our first time here…

Why we chose to come here at this time of the year…

Interesting things we saw on our way here…

The terrain we covered… The cost of gas…

What was the weather like? Breezy or calm?

Where we are staying, why we chose to stay here… The view from our window…

The cost per night, the sleeping arrangements…

Another place or two that we might want to consider staying next time…

We ate out or made our own recipes...

How we spent our days...

Describe the sights, sounds, and "the feel" of the place.

I'm glad I remembered to bring... Next time I don't want to forget...

The next time we come here we would like to...

Momentos or souvenirs we brought home...

The ride home...

MEXICAN GOLD POPPY, PICACHO PEAK STATE PARK, These poppies are usually in full bloom during the warm spring months.

What I will remember most about this getaway…

I can't change the direction of the wind, but I can adjust my sails.

—ANONYMOUS

FALL COLORS IN TRANSEPT CANYON, GRAND CANYON NATIONAL PARK The North Rim is located three and a half hours north of Flagstaff, and it provides an amazingly different view of the Grand Canyon. The colors during the fall are spectacular.

Recall it as often as you wish,
a happy memory never wears out.
—LIBBIE FUDIM

Date_____ Day of the week_____

Time we left_____ Time we arrived_____

Time we left for home_____ Time we returned_____

Today our destination is…

Why we chose to vacation here…

We have been here before or this is our first time here…

How we heard about this place… Why we chose to come here at this time of the year…

Interesting things we saw on our way here…

The terrain we covered… The cost of gas…

What was the weather like? Blue skies or cloudy?

Beautiful sunrises, fiery red sunsets, starry nights…

MOUNTAIN WILDFLOWERS, LITTLE COLORADO RIVER Springtime abounds with color near the Little Colorado River.

Flowers always make people better, happier,
and more helpful; they are sunshine, food,
and medicine to the soul.

—LUTHER BURBANK

Culinary delights we had for breakfast, lunch, or dinner...

Where we are staying, why we chose to stay here... The view from our window...

The cost per night, the sleeping arrangements...

Another place or two that we might want to consider staying next time...

Describe the sights, sounds, and "the feel" of the place.

How we spent our days...

LICHEN COVERED SPRUCE AND GAMBLE OAK, MORMAN MOUNTAIN Lichen covers these trees all year-round, but the best time to visit the Mountain is in the fall when the leaves turn brilliant colors.

Nature will reveal her secrets to us if we only
take the time to sit still, observe, and listen.
—Linda Kranz

Arizona's vast forestlands are a rich natural asset.
—Joseph Garrison Pearce

I'm glad I remembered to bring… Next time I don't want to forget…

The next time we come here we would like to…

Momentos or souvenirs we brought home…

The ride home…

ROCK FORMATION, BLUE MESA, PETRIFIED FOREST NATIONAL PARK The Park is located east of Holbrook just off I-40. Follow the paved road through the park any time of year in order to take in the sweeping vistas.

What I will remember most about this vacation…

Once my heart planted itself in the dry, salty earth called Sonoran Desert, it sprouted roots that I don't think could have anchored themselves in any congested city… I now spend days on end talking only to spindly cactus and spiny shrubs.

— GARY PAUL NABHAN

Put your own photos here or draw something you want to remember.

ASPEN GROVE AND WILDFLOWERS, SAN FRANCISCO PEAKS This road is located a short distance north of Flagstaff. Summertime drives offer views of beautiful green fields and tall stands of ponderosa pine trees.

The perfect journey is circular—the joy of
departure and the joy of return.
— DINO BASILI

Date _____ Day of the week _____

Time we left _____ Time we arrived _____

Time we left for home _____ Time we returned _____

Today our destination is…

Why we chose to vacation here…

We have been here before or this is our first time here…

How we heard about this place… Why we chose to come here at this time of the year…

Interesting things we saw on our way here…

The terrain we covered… The cost of gas…

Describe the sights, sounds, and "the feel" of the place.

SAGUARO CACTUS, SAGUARO NATIONAL PARK WEST, TUCSON
You can view these spectacular cactus all year-round, but they
are especially beautiful when they are in bloom.

What was the weather like? Blue skies or cloudy?

Beautiful sunrises, fiery red sunsets, starry nights…

How we spent our days…

ASPENS IN FALL COLOR, LOCKETT MEADOW, FLAGSTAFF This area, located about twenty-five minutes north of Flagstaff, offers hikers and campers plenty of opportunities to explore.

No sight is more provocative of
awe than is the night sky.
—LLEWELYN POWYS

Mountains are the beginning and
the end of all natural scenery.
—JOHN RUSKIN

We ate out or made our own recipes…

Where we are staying, why we chose to stay here… The view from our window…

The cost per night, the sleeping arrangements…

Another place or two that we might want to consider staying next time…

LOWER ANTELOPE CANYON, PAGE Located just north of Page, this canyon is well worth taking the time to see. Just make sure that you avoid the canyons during the summer monsoon season.

Put your own photos here or draw something you want to remember.

Momentos or souvenirs we brought home...

The next time we come here we would like to...

STRAWBERRY HEDGEHOG CACTUS, BLACKFOOT DAISIES, AND NEEDLELEAF DOGWEED, BEAVER CREEK The best times to see this beautiful flora in bloom is during the late spring months.

I'm glad I remembered to bring... Next time I don't want to forget...

The ride home...

What I will remember most about this vacation…

Nothing prepares you for the Grand Canyon. No matter how many times you read about it or see it pictured, it still takes your breath away. Your mind, unable to deal with anything on this scale, just shuts down and for many long moments you are a human vacuum, without speech or breath, but just a deep, inexpressible awe that anything on this earth could be so vast, so beautiful, so silent.

—BILL BRYSON

SUNSET CRATER VOLCANO, SUNSET CRATER NATIONAL MONUMENT Only twenty minutes north of Flagstaff, this national monument offers a close up view of a lava flow. Wildflowers dot the scenery during early spring, and full fields of flowers appear in late summer.

Arizona. Mellow, golden, sustaining, beautiful…
I tell you, this is a wonderful country.
                                                        —ZANE GREY

A Check List

- ___ Map
- ___ Comfortable shoes
- ___ Sunscreen
- ___ Hat
- ___ Light jacket or sweater
- ___ Rain gear
- ___ Camera and extra film
- ___ Snacks
- ___ Thermos with hot water for coffee or tea
- ___ Water or other beverages
- ___ Sunglasses
- ___ Bug repellent
- ___ Binoculars
- ___ Addresses and stamps for postcards
- ___ Passes for State Parks and National Monuments

___ _____
___ _____
___ _____
___ _____
___ _____
___ _____
___ _____
___ _____
___ _____
___ _____
___ _____
___ _____
___ _____
___ _____
___ _____

Arizona Climate Chart

DESERT REGION	High	Low	MOUNTAIN REGION	High	Low
January	66	37	January	50	21
February	69	39	February	54	24
March	75	42	March	58	27
April	83	49	April	67	34
May	92	56	May	76	40
June	100	65	June	84	47
July	100	73	July	89	57
August	98	71	August	85	55
September	96	66	September	82	48
October	87	54	October	72	37
November	75	43	November	59	27
December	67	38	December	51	22

Temperatures are in Fahrenheit

Sunrise & Sunset Chart

Date	Sunrise	Sunset	Date	Sunrise	Sunset
January 1	7:35	5:24	July 9	5:19	7:43
January 22	7:32	5:41	July 23	5:28	7:37
February 5	7:22	5:57	August 6	5:38	7:25
February 19	7:08	6:11	August 20	5:49	7:10
March 5	6:51	6:24	September 3	5:59	6:51
March 19	6:32	6:36	September 17	6:10	6:31
April 2	6:12	6:47	October 1	6:20	6:11
April 16	5:53	6:59	October 15	6:31	5:52
April 30	5:36	7:10	October 29	6:44	5:35
May 14	5:23	7:21	November 12	6:57	5:23
May 28	5:14	7:32	November 26	7:11	5:15
June 11	5:11	7:40	December 10	7:23	5:14
June 25	5:13	7:44	December 24	7:32	5:19

The times reflected on this chart are calculated for Northern Arizona, so other areas of the state might find as much as a 7 minute difference in the times shown above. Also, most areas in Arizona do not follow Daylight Savings Time, and therefore, these times are based on Mountain Standard Time and Pacific Standard Time depending on the time of year.

There is so much in the world for us all if we only have the eyes to see it, and the heart to love it, and the hand to gather it to ourselves.

—LUCY MAUD MONTGOMERY

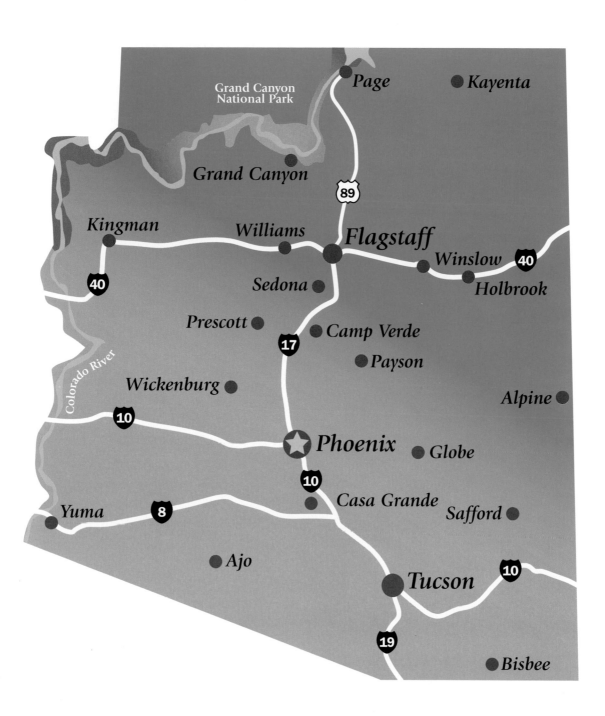

Arizona State Map

Resources

Arizona Office of Tourism
2702N. Third Street, Ste. 4015
Phoenix, AZ 85004
(800) 842-8257, (602) 230-7733
www.arizonaguide.com

Arizona State Parks Office
1300 West Washington, Suite 104
Phoenix, AZ 85007
(800) 285-3703, (602) 542-4174
(602) 542-4180 fax
www.pr.state.az.us

**Arizona Association of
Bed and Breakfast Inns**
P.O. Box 22086
Flagstaff, AZ 86002-2086
(800) 284-2589
www.arizona-bed-breakfast.com

ARIZONA CHAMBERS
OF COMMERCE

Alpine Chamber of Commerce
P.O. Box 410
Alpine, AZ 85920
(928) 339-4330
(928) 339-1887 fax
chamber@alpine-az.com
www.apline-az.com

Bisbee Chamber of Commerce
P.O. Box BA
Bisbee, AZ 85603
(520) 432-5421
(520) 432-3308 fax
chamber@bisbee.arizona.org
www.bisbee.arizona.org

**Cottonwood & Verde Valley
Chamber of Commerce**
1010 S. Main Street
Cottonwood, AZ 86326
(520) 634-7593
(520) 634-7594 fax
cottonwoodchamber@sedona.net
www.chamber.verdevalley.com

Flagstaff Chamber of Commerce
101 W. Route 66
Flagstaff, AZ 86001
(800) 842-7293, (928) 774-4505
(928) 779-1209 fax

dmaurer@flagstaff.az.us
www.flagstaff.az.us

Fredonia Chamber of Commerce
P.O. Box 547
Fredonia, AZ 86022
(928) 643-7241
(928) 643-7627 fax

**Grand Canyon
Chamber of Commerce**
P.O. Box 3007
Grand Canyon, AZ 86023
(928) 638-2901
www.grandcanyonchamber.com

Holbrook Chamber of Commerce
100 E. Arizona
Holbrook, AZ 86025
(800) 524-2459, (928) 524-6558
(928) 524-1719 fax
holbrookchamb@cybertrails.com

Jerome Chamber of Commerce
P.O. Drawer K
Jerome, AZ 86331
(928) 634-2900
(928) 634-5477 fax
www.jeromechamber.com

Kayenta Chamber of Commerce
P.O. Box 187
Kayenta, AZ 86033
(928) 697-3463
(928) 697-8553 fax

**Lake Havasu City
Chamber of Commerce**
314 London Bridge Road
Lake Havasu City, AZ 86403
(520) 855-4115
(520) 680-0010 fax
GaryLP@aol.com
www.havasuchamber.com

**Nogales-Santa Cruz
Chamber of Commerce**
123 W. Kino Park
Nogales, AZ 85621
(520) 287-3685
(520) 287-3688 fax
beth@nogaleschamber.com
www.nogaleschamber.com

**Page & Lake Powell
Chamber of Commerce**
P.O. Box 727
Page, AZ 86040
(928) 645-2741
(928) 645-3181 fax
chamber@pagelakepowellchamber.org
www.pagelakepowellchamber.org

Phoenix Chamber of Commerce
201 North Central Avenue, Suite 2700
Phoenix, AZ 85004
(602) 254-5521
(602) 495-8913 fax
info@phoenixchamber.com
www.phoenixchamber.com

**Pinetop, Lakeside, Greer, &
Show Low Chamber of Commerce**
102-C W. White Mountain Blvd.
Lakeside, AZ 85929
(928) 367-4290
(928) 367-1247 fax
plcofc@whitemtns.com
www.pinetop.com

Prescott Chamber of Commerce
P.O. Box 1147
Prescott, AZ 86302-1147
(928) 445-2000
(928) 445-0068 fax
chamber@prescott.org
www.prescott.org

Rim Country Chamber of Commerce
P.O. Box 1360
Payson, AZ 85547
(928) 474-4515
(928) 474-8812 fax
rcrc@rimcountrychamber.com
www.rimcountrychamber.com

Scottsdale Chamber of Commerce
7343 Scottsdale Mall
Scottsdale, AZ 85251
(480) 945-8481
(480) 947-4523 fax
info@scottsdalechamber.com
www.222.scottsdalechamber.com

**Sedona & Oak Creek
Chamber of Commerce**
P.O. Box 478
Sedona, AZ 86339
(928) 204-1123
(928) 204-1064 fax

info@sedonachamber.com
www.sedonachamber.com

Tombstone Chamber of Commerce
P.O. Box 995
Tombstone, AZ 85638
(520) 457-9317
(520) 457-2458 fax
tombstonechamber@theriver.com
www.tombstone.org

Tucson Chamber of Commerce
P.O. Box 991
Tucson, AZ 85702
(520) 792-1212
(520) 882-5704 fax
center@azstarnet.com
www.tucsonchamber.org

Williams & Grand Canyon Chamber of Commerce
200 W. Railroad Avenue
Williams, AZ 86046
(928) 635-4061
(928) 635-1417 fax
info@williamschamber.com
www.williamschamber.com

NATIONAL PARKS & MONUMENTS

Canyon de Chelly National Monument
P.O. Box 588
Chinle, AZ 86503-0588
(928) 674-5500

Casa Grande Ruins National Monument
1100 Ruins Drive
Coolidge, AZ 85228-3200
(520) 723-3172

Chiricahua National Monument
Dos Cabezas Route
Box 6500
Wilcox, AZ 85643-9737
(520) 824-3560

Coronando National Memorial
4101 East Montezuma Canyon Road
Hereford, AZ 85615-9376
(520) 366-5515

Fort Bowie National Historic Site
P.O. Box 158
Bowie, AZ 85605-0158
(520) 847-2500

Glen Canyon National Recreation Area
P.O. Box 1507
Page, AZ 86040-1507
(928) 608-6200

Grand Canyon National Park
P.O. Box 129
Grand Canyon, AZ 86023-0129
(928) 638-7888

Lodging at the Grand Canyon, North Rim
(800) 365-2267, (303) 297-2757
(303) 297-3175 fax

Lodging at the Grand Canyon, South Rim
Same day reservations (928) 638-2631
Advance reservations (303) 297-2757

Hubbell Trading Post National Historic Site
P.O. Box 150
Ganado, AZ 86505-0150
(928) 755-3475

Montezuma Castle National Monument
P.O. Box 219
Camp Verde, AZ 86322 0219
(520) 567-3322

Navajo National Monument
H.C. 71, Box 3
Tonalea, AZ 86044-9704
(928) 672-2366

Organ Pipe Cactus National Monument
Route 1, Box 100
Ajo, AZ 85321-9626
(520) 387-6849

Petrified Forest National Park
P.O. Box 2217
Petrified Forest, AZ 86028-2217
(928) 524-6228

Pipe Springs National Monument
H.C. 65, Box 5
Fredonia, AZ 86022
(928) 643-7105

Saguaro National Park
3693 S. Old Spanish Trail
Tucson, AZ 85730-5699
(520) 733-5153

Sunset Crater Volcano National Monument
6400 N. Highway 89
Flagstaff, AZ 86004
(928) 526-0502

Tonto National Monument
H.C. 02, Box 4602
Roosevelt, AZ 85545
(520) 467-2241

Tumacacori National Historic Park
P.O. Box 67
Tumacacori, AZ 85640-0067
(520) 398-2341

Tuzigoot National Monument
P.O. Box 219
Camp Verde, AZ 86322-0219
(928) 634-5564

Walnut Canyon National Monument
6400 N. Highway 89
Flagstaff, AZ 86004
(928) 526-3367

Wupatki National Monument
6400 N. Highway 89
Flagstaff, AZ 86004
(928) 679-2365

About the Author and Photographer

LINDA AND KLAUS KRANZ have been residents of Arizona for
over twenty-eight years. They have always enjoyed exploring
and discovering new areas of the state. Day trips and weekend
getaways are what keep them enthusiastic about their Monday
through Friday routines. They live in Flagstaff, Arizona with
their daughter Jessica and son Nik. This is the fourth journal
they have created together.

OTHER NORTHLAND PUBLISHING BOOKS
BY LINDA KRANZ:

All About Me: A Keepsake Journal for Kids
More About Me: Another Keepsake Journal for Kids
Through My Eyes: A Journal for Teens
For My Child: A Mother's Keepsake Journal
A Father's Journal: Memories for my Child
Expecting You: My Pregnancy Journal (FISHER BOOKS)